IMAGES
of America

GERMAN CINCINNATI
REVISITED

ON THE COVER: The Deutscher Jugendchor of Cincinnati was founded by the German-American Citizens League of Greater Cincinnati in 1935 and was directed by Wilhelm Kappelhoff (left of center). Kappelhoff was the father of Doris Kappelhoff, who would become Doris Day. (Courtesy of the author.)

IMAGES
of America

GERMAN CINCINNATI
REVISITED

Don Heinrich Tolzmann

ARCADIA
PUBLISHING

Copyright © 2011 by Don Heinrich Tolzmann
ISBN 9781531655167

Published by Arcadia Publishing
Charleston, South Carolina

Library of Congress Control Number: 2010943218

For all general information, please contact Arcadia Publishing:
Telephone 843-853-2070
Fax 843-853-0044
E-mail sales@arcadiapublishing.com
For customer service and orders:
Toll-Free 1-888-313-2665

Visit us on the Internet at www.arcadiapublishing.com

*Adopt the best parts of the American spirit and melt
these with the best parts of the German spirit.*

—*Carl Schurz*

CONTENTS

ACKNOWLEDGMENTS

Thanks to my son, Christian Heinrich, and my wife, Patricia, for their assistance in completing this work. Unless otherwise noted, the images in this volume are photographs the author has taken or are from his private collection.

—Don Heinrich Tolzmann
Cincinnati, Ohio

INTRODUCTION

German Cincinnati Revisited illuminates the major festivities, celebrations, and programs throughout the calendar year in the Greater Cincinnati area that relate to and reflect the German heritage of the region. The text begins with the celebration of Bockfest in March, heralding the end of winter and the beginnings of spring, and continues with chapters on Maifest, German Day, RoeblingFest, Schuetzenfest, Oktoberfest, and German-American Heritage Month. Several daughter settlements established by German Americans from Cincinnati are also surveyed, and a final chapter provides information about the German Heritage Museum, where further information can be found regarding the history and heritage of the German element of the region.

This title complements my earlier volume, *German Cincinnati* (Arcadia Publishing, 2005), which provides an illustrated history of German Americans in the Greater Cincinnati area with chapters titled Images and Symbols; Immigration and Settlement; Religious Life; Social Life; Education, Business, and Industry; Cultural Contributions; Newspapers, Journals, and Authors; War and Politics; and the German Heritage Revival.

German Cincinnati Revisited concentrates on the major German heritage events as they transpire throughout the calendar year, bringing German customs and traditions more vividly into focus and illustrating how they reflect and define the German heritage of the region.

One

BOCKFEST AND BIERKULTUR

The annual celebration of Bockfest in Cincinnati began in 1992, but the festival has much older origins, reaching back to medieval times in Germany. The word *bock* is German for "goat." Bock beer is, therefore, often associated with images of goats, and a number of legends and myths have arisen connecting goats to the brew. However, the origins of this beer actually have nothing to do with goats, as the name derives from the city where the brew originated—Einbeck, in what is today Lower Saxony in northern Germany. Here, this robust lager beer was first brewed in the 13th century.

Bock beer was traditionally brewed during the Lenten season because it was a hearty brew that was not restricted during Lent as it was considered "liquid bread." Due to this, bock beer came to be associated with the end of winter and the onset of spring, and many of the breweries brought out their bock beer at this time. This led to the idea of starting an annual Bockfest to celebrate the changing of these seasons and the German brewing heritage of the old Over-the-Rhine district.

Every year, Bockfest in Cincinnati has its official beginning on a Friday afternoon, when a goat pulling the ceremonial first keg of bock beer leaves Arnold's Bar and Grill, Cincinnati's oldest saloon, and pulls it down Main Street into Over-the-Rhine. A Bockfest parade follows, led by an honorary parade marshal, and concludes with the blessing of the beer at Bockfest Hall by a Franciscan priest.

This chapter highlights Bockfest and the German brewing heritage of the Greater Cincinnati area. Additionally, it provides a historical overview of some of the great German restaurants and beer gardens of the area. Taken together, these things help explain why Bockfest is celebrated annually in Cincinnati and why *Bierkultur* has become an integral part of the area.

This Brewery District historical marker is located in the Over-the-Rhine District at 231 West McMicken Avenue. It pays tribute to the German brewing heritage of the area; most of the city's 36 breweries were located in the Over-the-Rhine district and the nearby West End. Still more breweries come into the equation when those in northern Kentucky and southeastern Indiana are taken into consideration.

OHIO HISTORICAL MARKER

CINCINNATI BREWERIES

The Brewery District contains the majority of Cincinnati's remaining breweries and associated structures such as icehouses, bottling buildings, offices, and stables. With the first brewery north of Liberty Street founded in 1829, German immigrants fueled the growth of the brewing industry; by 1891, Cincinnati breweries produced over four barrels of beer per resident annually, almost twice as much as any other city in the nation. The brick breweries were typically designed in the Romanesque Revival style, and larger complexes often covered multiple city blocks. To produce the lager style beer common by 1860, typically very deep basements were dug or tunnels were cut into hillsides for the lagering process. At the height of production, 18 of the 36 breweries in greater Cincinnati were operating in Over-the-Rhine and the West End. Prohibition in 1919 closed most of the breweries permanently.

THE BREWERY DISTRICT COMMUNITY URBAN REDEVELOPMENT CORP
2008   THE OHIO HISTORICAL SOCIETY   72-31

The Christian Moerlein Brewing Company was headquartered on Elm Street in the northwest section of the Over-the-Rhine district, just north of Findlay Market, and was established by Christian Moerlein. The majestic Moerlein brew house (1868), on the northeast corner of Elm and Henry Streets, unfortunately was torn down in 1947.

Christian Moerlein (1818–1897) was born in the village Truppach in Upper Franconia and came to America in 1841, arriving in Cincinnati in 1842. In 1853, he joined Adam Dillmann in starting a brewery, which brought out its first beer in 1854. The next year, Dillmann died, and Moerlein partnered with Conrad Windisch. He stayed in business with Windisch until 1866, when he bought out Windisch's share.

Christian Moerlein's son George (1852–1891) was the crown prince of the family-centered brewing company. After studies at the Brewing Academy in Nürnberg, George served as vice president of the company. He helped create the image of the flashy and flamboyant beer baron.

In 1884–85, George Moerlein undertook a trip around the world and in 1886 the M. & R. Burgheim Publishing Company of Cincinnati published his travel account in English as *A Trip Around the World* and in German as *Eine Reise um die Welt*. A reviewer described Moerlein as "a deep thinker and an earnest student . . . it is a pleasure to see a busy, brainy man like Mr. Moerlein, who in spite of tremendous business, can still find time for scholarly pursuits."

Barbarossa was one of the popular beers brewed by the Christian Moerlein Brewing Company and was advertised as "the finest in the world." The advertisement emphasized that it was "brewed from the best hops and malt" and that it was an "unsurpassed family beer."

In 1863, Johann Hauck (1828–1896) joined with Johann Ullrich Windisch to found the Hauck and Windisch Company on Dayton Street in the West End. After Windisch's death, the brewery was reorganized in 1881 as the John Hauck Brewing Company. Their brew acquired a reputation as one of the premium beers of the area.

This advertisement noted that Hauck's beer was "from the finest malt and the most select hops." It also highlighted its brews—Golden Eagle, Imperial, and Special Dark.

Conrad Windisch (1825–1887), the son of a brewer in Egloffstein, Bavaria, came to America after the Revolutions of 1848. In Cincinnati, he found work at Herancourt's Brewery and then at the Koehler & Company Brewery. From 1854 to 1866, he partnered with Christian Moerlein and then launched the Löwen-Brauerei, or Lion Brewery, together with Gottlieb and Heinrich Mühlhäuser, which developed into one of the major breweries of the area.

Lion Beer, or Löwenbrau, was an especially popular brew. The brewing complex was huge and strategically located along the Miami Erie Canal, better known among locals as the Rhine. Its architectural style typified German American breweries, which used a Romanesque style known as *Rundbogenstil* (round-arch style).

CHAS. F. WINDISCH

Hughes High School

Bibliothek

CINCINNATI   OHIO

Cincinnati's German American brewers were well known for their generous contributions to philanthropic projects in the community. For example, Charles Windisch (1864–1939), the son of Conrad Windisch and husband of Amanda Mühlhäuser, donated a German encyclopedia to the library of Hughes High School.

Gottlieb Mühlhäuser (1836–1905) was born in Muggendorf, Bavaria, and came to America with his family, settling in Portsmouth, Ohio. In 1854, he started a mineral water business with his brother Heinrich, selling it in 1859 to start a highly profitable flour mill. Thereafter, Mühlhäuser and his brother joined Conrad Windisch to start the Löwen-Brauerei, learning brewing from Windisch, whose sister he had married in 1857.

Heinrich Mühlhäuser (1842–1914), the younger brother of Gottlieb, was born on the family farm in Portsmouth, Ohio. Working closely with his brother in business ventures that finally led to both partnering with Windisch, they exemplify the family-run businesses that were characteristic of German American breweries.

Foss-Schneider represents another Cincinnati German brewery whose beautiful building complex is no longer extant.

Klinckhamer Apartment Building, on the corner of Thirteenth and Race Streets in Over-the-Rhine, was built where the Park Brewery once stood. It was so named because it was across from Washington Park. The brewery (1860–1896) was founded by Joseph Niehaus (1819–1887) and Heinrich Klinckhamer (1825–1888).

Joseph Niehaus was Heinrich Klinckhamer's partner in owning the Park Brewery. Like other breweries, this one was located close to the former canal, now Central Parkway. After the demise of its founding fathers, the next generation apparently did not want to continue the business (the son of Joseph Niehaus was the secretary of the National Hardware Company), and so it closed.

Louis Hudepohl (1842–1902) was born in Cincinnati of north German stock, his family coming from north of Osnabrück. In 1885, he and George H. Kotte acquired the Buckeye Brewery, which became a major brewery in the area. After the death of his partner, Hudepohl reorganized the brewery in 1900 as the Hudepohl Brewing Company.

GEORG WIEDEMANNN.

Georg Wiedemann (1833–1890) was from Eisenach in Sachsen-Weimar in Thüringen, proving that not all beer barons were Bavarians. He came to America in 1854, first working at breweries in New York, Louisville, and Cincinnati. In 1870, he moved to Newport, Kentucky, where he partnered with a friend to start the Butscher & Wiedemann Brewery. In 1878, he bought out his partner and formed the Wiedemann Brewery.

The John Brenner Brewing Company was established in 1840 in Covington, and this building was constructed in 1895. Before Prohibition, it produced 50,000 barrels of beer annually.

The Deutsche Gastwirtschaft of Christian Sachs was a popular restaurant and bar located at Findlay Market on Elder Street. It was the meeting place for more than a dozen German American societies, including the Bayerischer Unterstützungs-Verein, or Bavarian Beneficial Society, which celebrated its 135th anniversary in 2010.

B. FLAMM'S

Deutſches Gaſthaus

Elder Straße und McMicken Ave.

Telephon: Canal 4617=Y.

B. Flamm, Eigentümer.

Die nachſtehenden Vereinigungen verſammeln ſich in obigem Lokal:

Allgemeiner Bäcker Gewerbe=Verein
Badiſcher Unterſtützungs=Verein
Cabinet Mutual Aid
Deutſcher Bund
Eintracht Stamm
Elſaß=Lothringer Damen=Zirkel
Elſaß=Lothringer Gegenſeitiger Unterſtützungs=Verein
Findlay Market Improvement Aſſociation
Frohſinn Loge, Deutſcher Orden der Harugari
Harmonie Stamm No. 280, U. O. R. M.
Huedepohl Männerchor
Jung's Militär=Kapelle
La Fraterne Club
Pocahontas Töchter; Metamora Stamm,
Star Building Aſſociation

Flamm's Deutsches Gasthaus on Elder Street and McMicken Avenue was another popular meeting place for local German American societies, including the Huedepohl Männerchor. On the hilltops overlooking the city were spacious beer gardens with dining, concert, and entertainment facilities. One of the most popular was the Bellevue House overlooking the Over-the-Rhine district, which it was connected to by means of the Bellevue Incline.

In 1883, *Harper's Magazine* reported that on summer evenings, German Americans would flock to the Bellevue House, listen to music, gaze at the river below, and enjoy "the excellent beer into which the German brewers transform annually so much of the water of the Ohio."

The Highland House was another of the beer gardens that overlooked the city from one of the hilltops.

MECKLENBURG'S GARDEN — CINCINNATI, OHIO — *Established 1865*

Mecklenburg's Gardens is located at East University and Highland Avenues and has the distinction of being the only German-style *Biergarten* to have survived Prohibition in Cincinnati, giving it a special historical ambience.

Featuring fine food and beverages, Mecklenburg's serves today as the meeting place of German societies, such as Schlaraffia and the German Mustard Club. Mecklenburg's also has a booth at certain festivities, including Oktoberfest Zinzinnati and, most recently, at the Bockfest.

Grammer's Restaurant at 1440 Walnut Street in Over-the-Rhine was established in 1872 by Anton Grammer (1832–1911) and became a meeting place for various German societies.

After his father's death in 1911, Frank Grammer (d. 1950), who started working at Grammer's Restaurant in 1887, took over the management. Born at the family home nearby on Liberty Street, Grammer strove to maintain the Gemütlichkeit that the restaurant was known for.

This *Bierdeckel,* or beer place mat, is from Grammer's Restaurant and is now a collector's item.

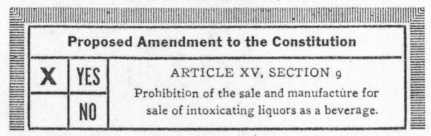

SEPARATE BALLOT
Marked for a Vote for State-Wide Prohibition
ELECTION NOVEMBER 6, 1917

		Proposed Amendment to the Constitution
X	**YES**	ARTICLE XV, SECTION 9
	NO	Prohibition of the sale and manufacture for sale of intoxicating liquors as a beverage.

OHIO DRY FEDERATION, J. A. WHITE, *Campaign Manager*, Columbus, Ohio

During World War I, a statewide vote on the question of Prohibition was placed on the election ballot. Prohibition forces exploited the anti-German hysteria and sentiment of World War I to urge voters to vote for Prohibition, claiming that brewers were pro-German and disloyal.

The Prohibition movement was aided by the remarks of US attorney general A. Mitchell Palmer, who stated that the brewing industry was "unpatriotic, because it has been pro-German in its sympathies." He went on to say that it was "owned by rich men, almost all of them are of German birth and sympathy" who supported "the organizations of this country [that] intended to keep young German immigrants from becoming real American citizens."

Are You a Loyal Citizen?

If You Are, You Cannot Vote to Maintain the Disloyal, Pro-German Beer Interests of Ohio

The United States is at war with Germany.

Uncle Sam says, "*I want your boy to fight in the trenches.*" You may not want to give your boy, but you bow to the will of the government, and your boy leaves home for the uncertainties of war.

Uncle Sam says to you, "*I want your money to help pay the expenses of this war,*" and he takes your money and your property to help make this country and the world safe for democracy. As patriotic citizens, you give your boy and your money to the public good.

Save! Save! Save!

Uncle Sam says we must conserve our grain and foodstuffs in this world crisis. We must feed our armies and furnish food for the hungry and starving of the other countries. "Aye!" "Aye!" is the general response.

The housewives are urged to save a slice of bread a day. "Save!" Save!" is the cry which is going up all over the land.

But the pro-German beer interests say, "*We will not save. We will go on wasting 3,390,000,000 pounds of foodstuff a year in the making of beer, and if you dare attempt to stop us, we will throttle legislation and not permit Congress to enact necessary war measures.*"

Now the same pro-German brewers are pleading with Ohio citizens to vote November 6 to approve their disloyalty and permit them to continue the waste of foodstuffs in the making of beer.

Tens of thousands of Germans here in Ohio, and elsewhere, are as much opposed to the plans of these pro-German brewers and as heartily in favor of the overthrow of beer autocracy as any class of people in this country. These Germans are good citizens, loyal Amer-

Restaurants like Grammer's had a tough time when Prohibition became the law of the land, and many of them closed for good. Fortunately, Grammer's not only survived but thrived due to its popularity.

25

Greg Hardman, the chief executive officer of the Christian Moerlein Brewing Company, celebrates at the 2009 Bockfest.

Manfred and Regina Schnetzer ride in the lead carriage for the 2010 Bockfest, with Manfred as parade marshal. (Courtesy of Manfred and Regina Schnetzer.)

Two

MAIFEST AND MUSIK

Since 1873, the Maifest, or May Festival, has been celebrated in Cincinnati and signifies the arrival of spring. In the old country, a *Maibaum*, or maypole, is often set up on the first of May, serving with its many colorful decorations as a symbol of the rebirth of nature.

By the 1870s, Anglo Americans noticed the great time the German singing societies had at their fests and decided to join forces with them. As a result, the first May Festival was held in May 1873. It was planned by an executive committee chaired by Col. George E. Nichols, who was assisted by his wife, Maria Longworth Nichols. The planning committee included Heinrich A. Rattermann, a well-known German American community leader.

The festival program had German composers and a German conductor, Theodor Thomas. A popular part of the May Festival was a direct loan from the German singing societies—the Sängerfest, during which all of the various choral societies, as well as the audience, joined together to sing in harmony.

In 1910, President Taft and the German ambassador, Count von Bernstorff, attended the May Festival. Toasts were presented to the president, his wife, the ambassador, and Germany. Many leading singers appeared at the May Festival, but the most popular was the great contralto Ernestine Schumann-Heink, who was well known for her popular Victrola recording of "Stille Nacht."

Today, the May Festival is still going strong at the music hall, built in part with funds donated by Reuben Springer, and an annual Maifest is held in the MainStrasse German Village in Covington. Some of the societies in the area sponsor Mayfest-related events, dinners, and dances, as well. More than one Maibaum can now be found in the Greater Cincinnati area.

In this chapter, the Maifest tradition is explored, as is the German musical heritage that made it possible for this fest to become the oldest annually celebrated event in the area.

The Männerchor maintained this hall at the corner of Vine and Mercer Streets in Over-the-Rhine. It was one of the larger German American singing societies in the 19th century.

In 1870, the Sänger-Halle was built across from Washington Park in Over-the-Rhine, where the music hall later was built.

The success of the early May festivals led to the idea of creating a more permanent structure to house the event. This resulted in the construction of the Musik-Halle, or music hall, which was dedicated in May 1878. Reuben R. Springer (1800–1884), a Kentuckian of German ancestry, promised to donate $125,000 if the people of Cincinnati would come up with an equal amount.

Henry Howe wrote the following in his *Historic Collections of Ohio*: "a distinguishing feature of the city has been her musical festivals, to be still greater, for she is to be the centre of music in this country."

Reuben R. Springer was born in 1800 in Frankfort, Kentucky, where his father, Karl Springer, son of German immigrants to Virginia, had moved after the American Revolution. A successful businessman, he became a strong advocate for the music hall after the third May Festival in 1877.

Since 1878, the music hall has been the home of the annual May Festival, the nation's oldest choral festival, which was conducted for many years by Theodore Thomas (1835–1905), its musical director.

Michael Brand directed the Cincinnati Grand Orchestra, which formed the foundation for the establishment of the Cincinnati Symphony Orchestra in 1895.

Michael Brand

Pike's Opera House was located on Fourth Street between Walnut and Vine Streets and had a large auditorium for musical performances and programs. Samuel Pike (Pike is the English translation of his German surname, Hecht), who was born in 1827 in Heidelberg, Germany, had become wealthy in the liquor business and opened the Opera House in 1859 in honor of Jenny Lind, the famous opera singer known as "the Swedish nightingale."

Heuck's Opera House was located on Twelfth and Vine Streets in Over-the-Rhine and was one of the major venues for popular music and entertainment in Cincinnati. Hubert Heuck (1834–1909) founded it.

Heuck's Opera House was known for its elegant interior and its top-of-the-line performers, who attracted huge audiences to its star-studded programs.

Many of the beer gardens, such as the Atlantic Garden, featured German music and had several musicians playing throughout the evening. On special occasions, larger orchestras were featured, performing works by some of the major composers.

Wielert's Pavilion on Vine Street was a favorite Over-the-Rhine saloon with a large beer garden. German bands, such as George Brand's orchestra, played German music, including Strauss and Volksmusik.

Churches published hymnbooks for use by their congregations, such as this one published by the Protestantischer Bund (Protestant Union). It was compiled by several ministers of Over-the-Rhine churches.

The Deutscher Literarischer Klub was founded in Cincinnati in 1877 and met at Grammer's Restaurant. Members held lectures on topics relating to German culture, and many of its members had published German-language works, especially literary and historical titles. As was common with German American societies, this one also had its own German songbook.

Fest Lieder

zur Feier des

GOLDENEN JUBILAEUMS

des

NORD AMERIKANISCHEN SAENGERBUNDES

(GEGRUENDET IN CINCINNATI IM JAHRE 1849.)

ABGEHALTEN IN

CINCINNATI, O.
1899.

LOUIS EHRGOTT ❖ FEST DIRIGENT.

THE JOHN CHURCH COMPANY,
CINCINNATI. ✛ NEW YORK, ✛ CHICAGO.
LEIPSIC.

In 1899, the Golden Jubilee of the national federation of German American singing societies, the Sängerbund, was celebrated in Cincinnati with John Goetz Jr. of the Christian Moerlein Brewing Company and Louis Hudepohl of the Hudepohl Brewing Company serving on the organizational committee.

Charles G. Schmidt (1851–1930) was known as "the Sängervater" as he served as president of the Nord-Amerikanischer Sängerbund, which planned and organized Sängerfeste across the country. Locally, he was president of the Vereinigte Sänger, or Combined Singers.

Emma Heckle (1855–1917) was one of the foremost Cincinnati German operatic singers of her time. In Bayreuth, she was the guest of Cosima Wagner. Returning to Cincinnati, she opened a music school on Fourth Street and often sang at the May Festival and at concerts sponsored by the Vereinigte Sänger.

The Jugendchor of the German-American Citizens League of Greater Cincinnati was directed in the 1930s by Wilhelm Kappelhoff (1892–1967), the father of actress Doris Day (b. 1924). He is pictured here seated in the first row, eighth from the right.

In 1948, Wilhelm Kappelhoff directed the Vereinigte Sänger for a program of German Christmas songs at Lytle Park, near the Taft Museum of Art. It was the first public event sponsored by them after World War II.

The Kolping Saengerchor was founded in 1989 by Carolann and James Slouffman with a group of 20 singers.

In 1999, the Kolping Saengerchor hosted the 150th anniversary of the National Sängerfest, celebrating the founding of the Sängerbund in Cincinnati in 1849.

PROGRAM BOOK

District Saengerfest

51st

Founding of N.A.S.B.
Anniversary

150th

Cincinnati Kolping Family
Anniversary

75th

May 14, 15, 16, 1999
KOLPING CENTER

"Singen Macht Freude"

Katie Hoffmann directs the Kinderchor of the Fairview German Language School during the opening ceremonies of the annual German Day celebration held at Findlay Market in Over-the-Rhine in 2010.

Mick Noll (right) gets ready to lead the parade for the annual Maifest in Covington, Kentucky, which has been held in the MainStrasse German Village since 1980. Well known for the active role he plays on behalf of German heritage, Noll has often been called "Mr. German Northern Kentucky." (Courtesy of Karin Albrecht.)

Gottfried Schlembach, a member of the Liberty Home German Society of Hamilton, Ohio, and the German-American Citizens League, enjoys some freshly tapped brew at the Covington Maifest in the MainStrasse German Village, an old German neighborhood featuring a Glockenspiel, German restaurants, and a variety of shops.

The Kindergruppe of the Donauschwaben Society of Cincinnati performs German folk dancing for the Maifest at the German Heritage Museum. (Courtesy of Franziska C. Ott.)

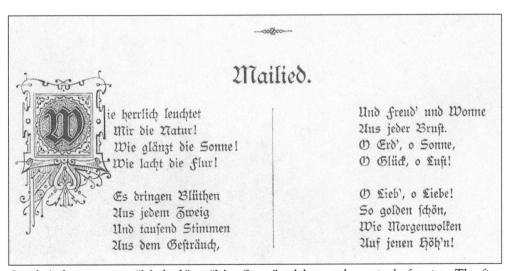

Mailied.

Wie herrlich leuchtet
Mir die Natur!
Wie glänzt die Sonne!
Wie lacht die Flur!

Es dringen Blüthen
Aus jedem Zweig
Und tausend Stimmen
Aus dem Gesträuch,

Und Freud' und Wonne
Aus jeder Brust.
O Erd', o Sonne,
O Glück, o Lust!

O Lieb', o Liebe!
So golden schön,
Wie Morgenwolken
Auf jenen Höh'n!

Goethe's famous poem "Mailied," or "May Song," celebrates the arrival of spring. The first stanza reads: "How gloriously nature glows unto me! How the sun beams, how the field laughs!" (author's translation).

Johann Wolfgang von Goethe (1745–1832), Germany's greatest author, is especially well known for his major work *Faust*, but he published many other memorable works, such as *The Sorrows of the Young Werther.*

A Maibaum has been erected at Germania Park, home of the Germania Society of Cincinnati.

Three

GERMAN DAY AND UNITY

German Day has been celebrated in Cincinnati since 1895 and is one of the oldest celebrations of its kind in the country. It was first organized by Heinrich A. Rattermann (1832–1923), the well-known German American historian who was the founder of the German Mutual Insurance Company, headquartered at the Germania Building at Twelfth and Walnut Streets in Over-the-Rhine.

The first German Day came about as a result of the 25th anniversary of the Battle of Sedan, the decisive battle during the Franco-Prussian War that led to the unification of Germany. The event was to be celebrated and combined with a celebration of German heritage in America. The theme for the festival, scheduled for the first of September, was German unity in the Old Country and German American unity in the New World. Ever since that time, German Day has been known as the Tag der Deutschen Einheit, or the Day of German Unity.

The event was such a huge success that it would be held annually as a celebration of German Day and the Deutsche Tag-Gesellschaft (German Day Society) was formed to coordinate plans. It was renamed the German American Alliance after joining the National German American Alliance, but after World War I, it changed its name to the Amerikanische Bürger-Liga, or American Citizens League, emphasizing American citizenship. Only after World War II did it reassert its identity by renaming itself the Deutsch-Amerikanische Bürger-Liga, meaning German American Citizens League, later adding "of Greater Cincinnati" to its name.

The German American Citizens League (GACL) continues to serve as the umbrella organization of the German American societies in the Greater Cincinnati area, including affiliates in the tristate region of Ohio, Kentucky, and Indiana. This chapter illuminates its history, showing the important role it has played on behalf of the German heritage of the region since it was established.

The annual German Day celebration begins with opening ceremonies and a parade at the historic Findlay Market in Over-the-Rhine.

German-American News
Deutsch-Amerikanische Nachrichten

VOLUME 16   2010   ISSUE 2

German Day Weekend

Saturday & Sunday, June 5 & 6, 2010 (11:00 a.m. To 11:00 p.m.)
Come Celebrate The Tri State's 115th Deutscher Tag

German Day Weekend Keg Tapping
Date: Wednesday, May 26 2010
Time: 7 p.m.
Location: Hofbräuhaus Newport

German Day Kickoff Parade
Date: Saturday, June 5 2010
Time: 11 a.m.
Place: Findlay Market

German Day Celebration
Date: Sunday, June 6 2010
Time: 11:00 a.m. - 11:00 p.m.
Place: Hofbräuhaus Newport

German-American
Citizens League of
Greater Cincinnati

German Day has expanded to a two-day celebration on the first weekend of June, beginning with the opening ceremonies and parade on Saturday at Findlay Market in Over-the-Rhine and continuing on Sunday at the Hofbräuhaus across the Ohio River in Newport, Kentucky.

Heinrich A. Rattermann (1832–1923) organized the first German Day in 1895. He was well known as the editor of the German American historical journal *Der Deutsche Pioneer* and as the author of numerous works dealing with German American history, literature, and culture.

After the celebration of the first German Day, John Goetz Jr. (1855–1899), second vice president of the Christian Moerlein Brewing Company, was elected president of the German Day Society. For the second German Day in 1896, Heinrich A. Rattermann was invited by Goetz as the main speaker for the celebration.

Judge August H. Bode (1845–1918) served as president of the German Day Society from 1900 to 1905, building the influence of the event and the organization's reputation in the community at large. He also was a member of the Cincinnati Turnverein and was considered one of the most influential members of the German American community.

In 1907, Judge John Schwaab (1855–1933) succeeded Judge Bode as president of the German Day Society, bringing about major changes. He led the move to affiliate the organization with the National German American Alliance, thus changing its name to the German American Alliance of Cincinnati. He held office as president until 1919, and in 1931, he was named honorary president.

Charlotte E. Neeb (1854–1956) was founder and first president of the Frauenstadtverband, or League of German American Women. Formed in 1910, it took an active role in beneficial and philanthropic affairs in the community and was a clearinghouse for job information for women.

Alban Wolff (1864–1938) was born in Nürnberg and ran a German and English printing firm in Covington, Kentucky, the Wolff Printing Company. He served as secretary of the German American Alliance of Covington and secretary of the German American Alliance of Kentucky.

American Citizens League

Ift der neue Name des deutsch-ameri-kanischen Stadtverbandes.

Präfident Schwaab erklärt in einer langen Rede warum der Name geändert werden follte.

Staats-Erefutive des D. A. Stadtverbandes wird angewiesen allen Lokal-verbänden nahe zu legen denselben Namen anzunehmen.

In an article in the *Cincinnatier Freie Presse*, Judge John Schwaab explained that the name of the German American Alliance would be changed to the American Citizens League (ACL) because the National German American Alliance would soon be dissolved as a result of the anti-German hysteria and sentiment engendered by World War I.

Henry Albertz (d. 1933) served as president of the ACL during the post–World War I years, from 1922 to 1932. Those years were difficult, as Prohibition meant festivals without "liquid bread." Albertz ran a German and English printing firm at 1308 Walnut Street and also served as secretary of the Mozart Loan and Building Association in Over-the-Rhine.

Eine deutsche Eiche faellt

Henry Gloeckler

The obituary of Henry Gloeckler (1878–1959), who served as president of the ACL from 1930 to 1947, was titled "Eine deutsche Eiche faellt," or "A German Oak Falls." He guided the ACL through the difficult times of the Great Depression and World War II. During the war, no German Day celebrations were held.

By the late 1930s, German Day celebrations at Coney Island attracted close to 40,000 people. Many people attended due to the fact that it was held at this amusement park, which was centrally located in the Greater Cincinnati area.

DEUTSCHER TAG

O du Heimat meiner lieber
Dein gedenk ich alle Zeit.

SONNTAG, AUGUST 21, 1932

CONEY ISLAND

Das 2:30 Boot wird begleitet vom Cincinnati Viking Klub.

Programm 4 bis 7 Uhr Abends

im MOONLIGHT GARDEN und HAUPTQUARTIER.

Programm Enthælt

Hartmann's Orchester.

Gruesse aus der Alten Heimat
Herr HENRY ALBERTZ, President der Buerger Liga.

Duning's Volkslieder Gruppe
Trachten Schau und Tanz geschichten aus dem wiener wald.

Vereinigte Sænger, Prof. Louis Ehrgott.

II. Teil

Ansprachen

Duning's Volkslieder Gruppe
Trachten Schau und Schwæbischer Volkstanz.
Unter leitung von Frau
Wilhelm - Kehrt Tanz Schule.

Turner Schau, Central Turngemeinde.

Weitere unterhaltung und gemuethliches Zusammensein im Hauptquartier.

A letter sent out by the ACL to all its member societies urges them to vote against the Anti-Saloon League candidates for Congress in the 1932 spring elections. Not until April 1933 was beer legal again in Cincinnati, and German festivities again thrived, including the annual German Day celebration.

Amerikanische Buerger-Liga

(AMERICAN CITIZENS LEAGUE)

Cincinnati, Ohio im April 1932.

An unsere Verbaende und Vereine,

Werte Herren:-

Am 10. Mai d. J., findet in unserem Staate die Vorwahl (Primary Election) statt. Und da die Prohibition neben der Arbeitslosigkeit eine der Hauptfragen in der gegenwaertigen Zeit ist, so moechten wir unsere Mitglieder und Freunde ganz besonders auf diese Wahl aufmerksam machen.

Die Anti-Saloon Liga hat Kandidaten fuer den Vereinigten Staaten Congress, sowie fuer den Staat Ohio aufgestellt, und wendet mit Hilfe der Frauen Organisationen alle Mittel an, um diesen Herren die Nomination zu sichern. Und haben diese Herren die Nomination, so wird es in der Hauptwahl einen schweren Kampf kosten diese Schuetzlinge der oben genannten Organisation zu schlagen.

Die ganze Nation wird ihr Augenmerk auf Ohio richten, und hoffentlich geben die Waehler den Fanatikern und ihrem Anhang in der Vorwahl am 10. Mai die richtige Antwort, indem sie die Kandidaten dieser Klicke zurueck weisen und nur fuer liberalgesinnten Maenner und Frauen stimmen.

Also kommt und thut Eure Pflicht; denn diese Vorwahl ist von ganz besonderer Wichtigkeit, da von derselben die Handlung des Ver. Staaten Congresses abhaengen wird.

Mit deutschem Gruss

HENRY ALBERTZ, Praesident   CHAS. E. MENIER, Sekretaer

Members of the Cincinnati Central Turners lead off the 1936 German Day Parade at Coney Island. The parade is an important part of the annual German Day celebration and includes representatives from the German societies of the area.

Jakob Herz (d. 1969) was a postwar immigrant from Hessen who served as president of the ACL from 1948 to 1953. His two major achievements were seeing to it that the American Citizens League was renamed the German American Citizens League (GACL) and also in organizing the first German Day celebration after World War II in 1948. Proceeds of the event went to war relief programs in Germany.

Katherine Grossheim (d. 1972) was the first and only woman ever elected GACL president, serving from 1955 to 1960. At this time, the GACL held its meetings at Steuben Hall in Clifton Heights, where it continued to meet until the 1990s.

52

Albert Landesvatter (1904–1992) served as GACL president from 1964 to 1971 and then as secretary until 1978. Due to his efforts, the GACL continued to grow and develop and attract additional member societies.

During the year of the American bicentennial in 1976, the GACL worked with the Cincinnati Public Library to sponsor an exhibit titled Prosit Cincinnati, which highlighted the contributions German Americans have made to the growth and development of the region.

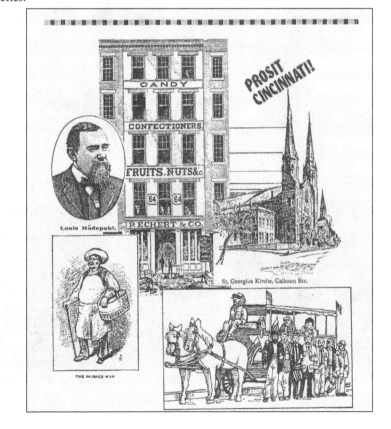

David Bitter (1936-2001) became GACL president in 1984 after serving as secretary, and he held office until 1994 (except for the year 1990). He cofounded the Cincinnati Sister Cities Association and played an important role in creating the Cincinnati-Munich sister city relationship. In 1988, he received the Federal Cross of Merit from the Federal Republic of Germany for his contributions to German American relations.

The Auswandererdenkmal, or Immigrants Monument, located in Bremerhaven, Germany, was supported by contributions from German American societies across the United States, including the GACL. The monument bears the GACL's name as a contributing organization.

In 1988, Cincinnati's bicentennial was celebrated, and the GACL organized programs designed to focus on the role German Americans have played in the growth and development of the city.

1788 - 1988
CINCINNATI BICENTENNIAL

Deutsch-Amerikanische Buerger-Liga
GERMAN AMERICAN CITIZENS LEAGUE
2357 Rohs Street, Cincinnati, Ohio 45219
established 1895

Gene Bertke (b. 1934) served as GACL president in 1990 after having served as vice president from 1985 to 1989.

Don Heinrich Tolzmann (b. 1945) was elected president of the GACL in 1995 and coordinated its 100th anniversary celebration in conjunction with the annual German Day festivities. Under his direction, the GACL opened the German Heritage Museum in September 2000 to showcase the history of German immigration, settlement, and influences in the region.

The year 1995 marked the 100th anniversary of the celebration of German Day in Greater Cincinnati, one of the oldest celebrations of its kind in the United States.

Cincinnati mayor Roxanne Qualls, GACL president Dr. Don Heinrich Tolzmann, and Franziska Ott Allen, chair of the GACL Public Affairs Committee, are pictured at the dedication of a historical marker on English Street, which was changed from German Street during the anti-German hysteria of World War I.

In 2001, the GACL dedicated a historical marker from the Ohio Historical Society, which was placed on the Cincinnati riverfront in honor of "Cincinnati's German Heritage."

OHIO
HISTORICAL
MARKER

CINCINNATI'S GERMAN HERITAGE
Cincinnati, along with Milwaukee and St. Louis, is one of the three corners of the "German Triangle," so-called for its historically high concentration of German-American residents. During the 19th century, Cincinnati was both a destination for immigrants to the tri-state area and a hub from which many groups of Germans moved inland to settle new Ohio communities — many along the Miami and Erie canal corridor which began here. German-Americans have greatly influenced the social, cultural, economic and political life of the Cincinnati area. At the turn of the 21st century, approximately half of Cincinnati's population was of German descent.
(Continued on other side)
THE OHIO BICENTENNIAL COMMISSION AND THE LONGABERGER COMPANY
GERMAN-AMERICAN CITIZENS' LEAGUE OF GREATER CINCINNATI
THE OHIO HISTORICAL SOCIETY
2001   22-31

In 2001, the GACL dedicated another historical marker, this one at Findlay Market, which dealt with the anti-German hysteria of World War I.

The German-American Citizens League
Of Greater Cincinnati
The Corporation for Findlay Market

**Anti-German Hysteria
Historical Marker Dedication**

June 4, 2005
11:00 am

At the opening ceremonies for German Day at Findlay Market, Marge Poole, GACL secretary and editor of *German American News*, recognizes officers and representatives of the German American societies of the area. (Courtesy of Shelley Drury.)

Four

ROEBLINGFEST AND REGION

Every June, the RoeblingFest in Covington, Kentucky, celebrates the John A. Roebling Suspension Bridge on the Ohio River. The bridge bears the name of its creator, John A. Roebling (1806–1869), who was born in Mühlhausen, Germany, studied engineering at the Royal Polytechnic Institute in Berlin, and attended lectures by notable philosopher Georg Wilhelm Friedrich Hegel.

With his brother Karl, he formed the Mühlhausen Immigration Society and led more than 50 immigrants to the United States in 1831. They founded the town of Saxonburg in Butler County, Pennsylvania, near Pittsburgh. There he produced his first wire rope, which he called "an assemblage of wires." He quickly learned English and in time wrote highly regarded articles on engineering topics. By the 1840s, he had built a reputation as a bridge- and aqueduct-builder of note.

The Covington and Cincinnati Bridge Company, which had been approved by the state legislatures of Kentucky and Ohio, selected Roebling to build a bridge on the Ohio River, which had been discussed for some time as desirable. Roebling surveyed the Ohio River site in 1846 but work did not begin until 10 years later, in 1856. After barely getting started, the financial panic of 1857 brought work to a halt.

Then, along came the Civil War, which meant that funding, building materials, and labor were in short supply or sometimes not available at all. The threat of invasion from the Confederate Army prompted the creation of a temporary pontoon bridge to transport troops to northern Kentucky for the defense of the area, convincing many that the real bridge had to be completed. The bridge was finally finished in late 1866, and it was dedicated on January 1, 1867.

Roebling's legacy resounds throughout the Ohio Valley to this day by means of the suspension bridge that he built on the Ohio River. It is not only a regional landmark, it is also in the National Register of Historic Places.

The Roebling Suspension Bridge serves as the major landmark of the region. Immigrants and settlers traveling on the Ohio River knew that when they caught sight of it, they had reached the Greater Cincinnati area.

After the American Revolution, settlers moved into the Ohio Valley, leading to the emergence of Cincinnati on the north side of the Ohio River and Covington and Newport, Kentucky, on the south side. The need for a bridge soon became clear, as ferryboats plied their way back and forth across the river with freight and passengers.

By the 1840s, the population of the region had grown to such an extent that the Covington and Cincinnati Bridge Company was formed. It invited John A. Roebling to survey the area in 1846.

Roebling issued a report on the possibilities of building a bridge for the Covington and Cincinnati Bridge Company. However, the company had been chartered only by the State of Kentucky (1846) and not that of Ohio. Finally, Ohio approved its charter in 1849, but with the provision that no Cincinnati Street could be in line with the bridge. This was stipulated to protect the business interests of Cincinnati.

John A. Roebling wrote a fascinating account of his immigration experience based on his diary, describing in detail his voyage from Bremerhaven to Philadelphia. The trip took nine weeks, lasting from May 23 to August 6, 1831. He also wrote of his initial experiences in America.

Diary of My Journey

from Muehlhausen *in* Thuringia *via* Bremen *to the* United States of North America

In the Year 1831

Written for my Friends

By Johann August Roebling

Printed in the Roebling Printing-House
Eschwege, 1832

⁓

Translated, with occasional notes,
from the original German

By EDWARD UNDERWOOD

With a Foreword

By HAMILTON SCHUYLER
Author: *The Roeblings, A Century of Engineers,*
Bridge Builders and Industrialists
1831-1931

⁓

PRIVATELY PRINTED BY THE ROEBLING PRESS
TRENTON, NEW JERSEY, 1931

During the Civil War, a pontoon bridge had to be built across the Ohio River so that Union forces could be brought to northern Kentucky to fortify and protect the area from the threat caused by the advancing Confederate troops, who were under the command of Gen. Edmund Kirby Smith.

Once the towers had been constructed, work could begin on spinning the cables, each of which is 12.5 inches thick and contains 5,180 wires.

After the cables were hung, 300 suspenders were fastened from them and attached to the bed of the bridge. A bed of oak and pine was laid in place.

Several carriages rolled across the Ohio Bridge when it was officially dedicated on January 1, 1867, the first one carrying John A. Roebling, engineer, and Amos Shinkle, president of the Covington Cincinnati Bridge Company.

Due to dams farther upstream, the Ohio River is much higher today than when the bridge was built. In the 19th century, the towers were on the banks of the river, rather than in the river, as they are today.

John A. Roebling viewed the Ohio Bridge as a stepping stone to his grand project—the Brooklyn Bridge. He died as a result of an accident in 1869 while working on that project; it had to be completed by his son Washington (1837–1920).

Washington Roebling served as assistant engineer for the final phase of construction of the Ohio Bridge and then went on to work on the Brooklyn Bridge, which was dedicated in 1883.

Henry C.P. Roebling (1835–1925) was the nephew of John A. Roebling and came to Cincinnati in 1856, most likely to help his uncle during the first phase of construction on the Ohio Bridge. He served in a Civil War regiment formed in Cincinnati, and after the war he resided in Delhi Township.

The bed of the bridge had to be built high enough to allow the passage of steamboats traveling on the Ohio River.

Amos Shinkle (1818–1892), president of the Covington and Cincinnati Bridge Company, was a highly successful businessman who became one of the wealthiest persons in the area by selling coal to steamboats on the Ohio River. He was born in Brown County, Ohio. His great-grandfather Philip Schenckel immigrated from the Rheinpfalz to Pennsylvania in the 18th century.

Shinkle's home in Covington is now an attractive bed and breakfast inn owned and operated by Bernie Moorman, former mayor of Covington.

Amos Shinkle's home was built in 1854 and reflected the success he had attained. Aside from selling coal to steamboats, his entrepreneurial accomplishments included the establishment of a bank, steamboat construction, gas lighting, and telephone service in Covington, and the building of more than 30 houses in Covington.

Shinkle donated funds for the construction of the Shinkle Methodist Church in Covington (1882). Noted for its Gothic architecture, the church features beautiful stained glass windows.

Amos Shinkle's son Bradford (1845–1892) succeeded his father as president of the Covington Cincinnati Bridge Company. Like his father, he was a successful businessman and served as president of the Champion Ice Company, donating to various philanthropic causes in the area.

Amos Clifford Shinkle was the grandson of Amos Shinkle and succeeded his father as president of the Covington and Cincinnati Bridge Company. Also a successful businessman, he served as president of the Cincinnati Central Trust and Safe Deposit Company.

During the flood of 1937, the Roebling Suspension Bridge was the only one to remain open on the entire Ohio River all the way from Steubenville, Ohio, to Cairo, Illinois.

This part of Covington, now known as Roebling Point, was inundated during the flood of 1937, but nevertheless, the bridge entranceway was kept open by means of sandbags.

The Covington and Cincinnati Bridge Company managed the Roebling Suspension Bridge until 1953, when it was acquired by the state of Kentucky for $4.2 million.

Although the bridge was officially dedicated on New Year's Day in 1867, work on it was completed late in 1866. As a result, the governors of Kentucky and Ohio celebrated the event on December 1, 1866, by meeting at the center of the bridge, where they exchanged salutations as a 100-gun salute was fired.

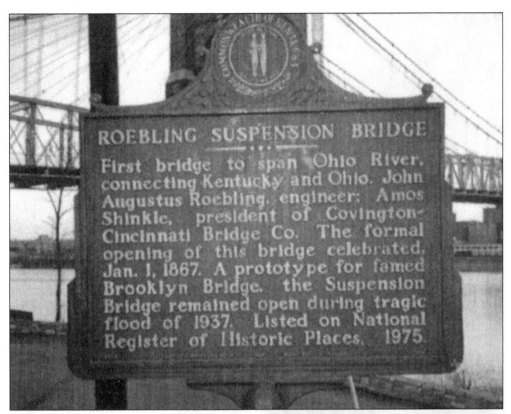

ROEBLING SUSPENSION BRIDGE

First bridge to span Ohio River, connecting Kentucky and Ohio. John Augustus Roebling, engineer; Amos Shinkle, president of Covington-Cincinnati Bridge Co. The formal opening of this bridge celebrated, Jan. 1, 1867. A prototype for famed Brooklyn Bridge, the Suspension Bridge remained open during tragic flood of 1937. Listed on National Register of Historic Places, 1975.

A historical marker on the Covington side of the bridge indicates that it was included in the National Register of Historic Places in 1975. In 1982, it also was declared a National Civil Engineering Landmark.

This bronze statue of Roebling in Trenton, New Jersey, where Roebling's company was located, reflects his firm resolve and determination.

The RoeblingFest is sponsored annually by the Covington-Cincinnati Suspension Bridge Committee, which was formed in 1975. Since 2010, it has cosponsored the fest with the Roebling Point Entertainment District.

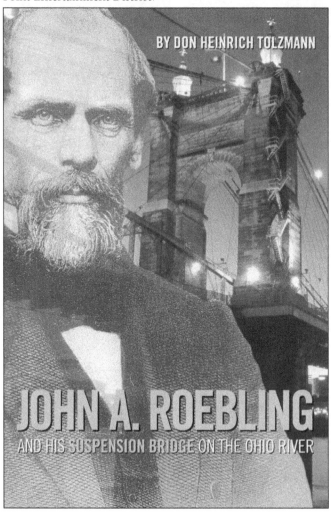

BY DON HEINRICH TOLZMANN

JOHN A. ROEBLING
AND HIS SUSPENSION BRIDGE ON THE OHIO RIVER

The author's *John A. Roebling and His Suspension Bridge on the Ohio River* (2007) provides a biography of Roebling, as well as a history of the bridge and its impact on the region.

Five

OLDEST AND
NEWEST FESTIVALS

Schuetzenfest is one of the oldest German festivals in the Greater Cincinnati area and has been celebrated annually in July by the Kolping Society of Cincinnati since the 1920s. However, its origins go back to 1866, when it was first introduced by the Cincinnati Schuetzen-Verein, or Cincinnati Sharpshooters Society, whose members were veterans of the Civil War. The society maintained its headquarters in Fairmount atop the hill that is now St. Clair Park, which overlooks what is now the Western Hills Viaduct. They held their target practice on the hill, which became known as the Schuetzenbuckel, or the Sharpshooters Hill.

The annual celebration of Oktoberfest is the most recent addition to the calendar of German festivals in the area. It has roots in a wedding anniversary party. On October 12, 1810, Crown Prince Ludwig of Bavaria, who later became King Ludwig I, married Princess Therese von Sachsen-Hildburghausen. The wedding party took place on a meadow outside the city walls of München, and since that time it has been known as the Theresienwiese, or Therese's meadow, as well as the Wies'n-Feld, or the meadow field. Everyone from München was invited, and at the conclusion of the celebration, a horse race was held as a festival event in honor of the entire kingdom of Bavaria.

The festival event developed from the decision to hold a horse race on an annual basis. Other elements were added to the event year by year. In 1811, the first agricultural exhibition was added to highlight the fall harvest in Bavaria. In 1818, the first carousel and two swings were set up, and visitors could obtain beer from small booths that were set up for their enjoyment. The numbers of attendees gradually began to increase with time.

With its strong German heritage, it is not surprising that the longest series of Oktoberfest celebrations in the United States takes place in the Greater Cincinnati area.

Fest-Zeitung

der

Norddeutschen Schützen-Gesellschaft.

SONNTAG, DEN 17. JUNI 1900.

This program of the Nordeutsche Schuetzen-Gesellschaft von Cincinnati, or North German Schuetzen Society of Cincinnati, provides information on the 16th annual Schuetzenfest. Before World War I, there were nine Schuetzenvereine in the area (seven in Cincinnati and two in Covington).

The North German Schuetzen Society of Cincinnati met at the West End Turner Hall, which was built in 1883 for the German American population of the area. John Hauck, who lived nearby on Dayton Street, served on the building committee of the West End Turnverein that oversaw construction of the hall.

August Kuhlmann served for eight terms as president of the Low German Schuetzen Society. The members of the Schuetzenvereine in the area were mainly from northern Germany and usually referred to themselves as low, or north, Germans.

This is the program of the 1910 Schuetzenfest of the Deutsche Schuetzen-Gesellschaft von Covington, or German Schuetzen Society of Covington, founded in 1882. When the Germania Hall was built in Covington in 1899, the society began holdings its meetings there, as did many of the German American societies of Covington.

Officers of the Deutsche Schuetzen-Gesellschaft, of Covington
1909-1910

JOHN P. HEIDEL,
President

H. H. REIHEMANN,
Vice-President

FRANK A. AVERBECK,
Secretary

HENRY JANSEN,
Treasurer

The Deutsche Schuetzen-Gesellschaft von Covington described itself as "a strictly German organization composed of Germans and those of German descent, and is organized to promote friendship and companionship."

LEWISBURG SCHUETZEN-GESELLSCHAFT

TURNER HALL
HOME LEWISBURG SCHUETZENS

KOENIG CARL VI

KOENIGIN JOSEPHINE

The Lewisburg Schuetzen-Gesellschaft held its meetings at Turner Hall in Covington, which is located just south of today's MainStrasse German Village.

St. Francis Church on Liberty Street in Over-the-Rhine became the home of the Kolping Society, which was founded in 1924. Rev. Maurice Ripperger, OFM, the pastor of the church, gave them permission to make use of the school for meetings.

In 1928, the newly formed Kolping Society acquired this hall on Republic Street (Bremen Street before World War I) in Over-the-Rhine. It had been a police station and was remodeled for use as the Kolping Haus, which was officially dedicated in 1930.

In 1953, the Kolping Society acquired land at 9158 Winton Road in Cincinnati, which became known as Kolping Grove and the site of the new Kolping Center. Aside from Schuetzenfest, many other festivities, programs, and dances were held here.

The Schuetzenclub of the Kolping Society takes part in the annual parade held during the Schuetzenfest at Kolping Grove. This annual parade also includes representatives of the German societies of the region.

Teams from the Schuetzenclub of the Kolping Society take part in shooting at a wooden eagle until the last piece is shot down by the marksman who becomes the Schuetzenkönig for the coming year.

The Kolping Band performs a concert of German music at the Schuetzenfest at Kolping Grove on Winton Road.

The annual Schuetzenfest takes place annually in July and is not only the oldest but also one of the largest German American festivals in the Greater Cincinnati area.

SCHUETZENFEST

Zinzinnati's Oldest Festival Since 1866

SUNDAY, JULY 22, 1990

Gate Opens 1:00 P.M.

Donation: $1.00   Children under 16 FREE

KOLPING GROVE

9158 WINTON ROAD
ADJOINING BRENTWOOD BOWL

OPENING PARADE & SHOOTING FOR KING 2:30 P.M.

DELICIOUS CHICKEN DINNERS

PLATZ KONZERT—FEATURING THE FAMOUS KOLPING ORCHESTRA

6:00 P.M. PARADE—CROWNING OF NEW KING AND QUEEN

BRATS • HOT DOGS • RIDES • BOOTH • GAMES

7:00 P.M. DANCING • POLKA DOTS

GRAND RAFFLE $1,000 CASH AWARD

SATURDAY: DANCE ONLY
JULY 21, 1990
9:00 P.M. 'til 1:00 A.M.

ZAPFENSTREICH AND DANCE
IN OUR PAVILION

Music by ALPEN ECHOES

Donation: $5.00 Adults – $3.50 Teens

WHAT IS THE SCHUETZENFEST?
Schuetzenfest is a traditional festival of the Catholic Kolping Society. A hand-carved eagle is used as a target for the marksmen. The individual to shoot the last part of the eagle has the honor of being proclaimed King for the year. All profits from the festival benefit the social, sports, and cultural sports exchanges, and myriad of charitable and philanthropic interests of the Catholic Kolping Society.

In 1992, the Kolping Society opened the new Kolping Center on Mill Road, where the Schuetzenfest and other events, activities, and programs of the society are held, such as concerts of the Kolping Saengerchor.

James and Carolann Slouffman reigned as Schuetzenkoenig and Schuetzenkoenigen from 1994 to 1995.

In 1971, the Germania Society of Cincinnati, which was founded in 1964, held the first Oktoberfest in the Greater Cincinnati area. In the beginning, the Germania Oktoberfest was held in Harvest Home Park in Cheviot, a west side suburb.

George Westendorf, pictured with wife Maria and daughter Susan, was chairman of Germania's first Oktoberfest in 1971 and later served as the society's president. (Courtesy of the Westendorf family collection.)

German music has always been an essential element in the celebration of Oktoberfest. (Courtesy of the Westendorf family collection.)

Early Oktoberfest celebrations honored an old Over-the-Rhine tradition of fetching beer in buckets and offered miniature souvenir cans to fest-goers. (Courtesy of the Westendorf family collection.)

Pictured from left to right are Gebhard Erler, host of the German radio program Deutsches Konzert, Holger Schwab, and George Frauendorfer, introducing a program at a Germania Oktoberfest at Harvest Home Park. (Courtesy of the Westendorf family collection.)

Eventually, the Germania Society moved the Oktoberfest to Germania Park on West Kemper Road in Colerain Township. Its *Klubhaus* was completed there in 1977, and Germania Park is the location of its meetings, functions, and festivities.

In 1976, the first Oktoberfest Zinzinnati was held in the city's downtown area on the recommendation of the German American Citizens League, which has been involved with the planning of the event ever since.

In the week before Oktoberfest Zinzinnati, the Gemuetlichkeit Games are held on Fountain Square, including the contest of racing across the square without spilling the beer from liter glasses held in both hands. Here, Marilyn Simon gets ready to carry a couple of beer steins across the square.

Herzlich Willkommen

Oktoberfest
Donauschwaben
··Cincinnati··

SOUVENIR PROGRAM

OCTOBER 2 - 3, 1993

The Donauschwaben Society also began sponsoring an annual Oktoberfest at its park grounds in Colerain Township on Dry Ridge Road.

Across the river from Cincinnati, Covington also began celebrating Oktoberfest with its event located in the MainStrasse German Village. The 32nd such festival was held in 2010.

Six

GERMAN-AMERICAN HERITAGE MONTH

Germans first arrived in America at Jamestown, Virginia, in 1608, and the 400th anniversary of their arrival was celebrated in 2008. Germans settled throughout the colonies, but especially in New York. However, it was not until 1683 that the first permanent all-German settlement was established in America by a group of 13 German families in Pennsylvania led by Franz Daniel Pastorius. On the October 6, they founded Germantown, which is now part of the city of Philadelphia. The settlement grew into the first German American center in what became the United States, and Philadelphia developed into the major port city for German immigration.

In 1883, the German American bicentennial of the founding of Germantown was celebrated in Philadelphia with a series of programs and celebrations, which included a guest lecture by Heinrich A. Rattermann, the well-known Cincinnati German historian and editor of the historical journal *Der Deutsche Pionier*. On his return home, Rattermann coordinated a similar celebration in Cincinnati. In 1908, the 225th anniversary of the founding of Germantown was widely celebrated across the country, including in Cincinnati, as was the 250th anniversary in 1933.

The declaration by President Reagan naming the sixth of October as German American Day in 1987 was widely celebrated nationally and appropriately in Cincinnati, where the idea and national campaign had begun. However, the event was only one day and did not provide enough time for a series of programs and related events. Therefore, the first German-American Heritage Month was organized in 1989, sponsored by the GACL of Greater Cincinnati. Proclamations have been obtained since that time from the governor of Ohio. German-American Heritage Month has also received the endorsement of a wide range of organizations in Ohio, including the Ohio Historical Society.

Since 1989, the GACL has planned and coordinated the celebration of October as German-American Heritage Month and encouraged its celebration nationwide.

The Pastorius Monument in Philadelphia honors Franz Daniel Pastorius (1651–1720) and the 13 German families who founded Germantown on October 6, 1683. (Courtesy of Robert Stocks.)

Eröffnungsrede bei Gelegenheit der Feier des Jubiläums der deutschen Einwanderung in Amerika.

Gehalten in Cincinnati am 17. Oktober 1883.

Verehrte Festgenossen, Damen und Herren!

Im Namen der Mitglieder des Anordnungs-Kommittees heiße ich Sie heute Abend hier in diesen festlichen Räumen willkommen! Mit dem Gruß des Mannes, dessen Name dieser Tage von rühmenden Lippen erklungen ist und noch erklingt im großen weiten Lande, vom Atlantischen bis zum Stillen Ozean und vom Golf von Mexiko bis zur Kette der großen Seen, mit dem Gruß dieses Mannes, der der Vorläufer war eines der wichtigsten Kulturelemente in der Zusammensetzung der amerikanischen Nation, Franz Daniel Pastorius, heiße ich Sie Alle hier willkommen:

„Heil deutsches Brudervolk in Amerika!"

Nicht hat er sich getäuscht, der edle Führer jener kleinen Schaar, die im Jahre 1683 auf dem Schiff „Concord" den Gestaden dieses Landes zueilte: groß und mächtig ist die Nachkommenschaft geworden in „Germanopolis". Nach Millionen und aber Millionen zählt sie, und gleich dem Samenkorn, das zu einem Riesenbaum wurde, breitet heute der Stamm des deutschen Brudervolkes seine Zweige aus über das ganze Land. Auf den Bergen und in den Thälern weilen die Söhne und Töchter Germaniens und die weitgestreckten Prairien sind von ihnen bevölkert worden. Die Grenzen von dem einst kleinen Germantown haben sich ausgebreitet, bis sie nunmehr größer sind, als das ganze alte Europa.

Wenn wir der Jubelfeiern gedenken, die heute über das weite Land dahinbrausen, wo überall Preis und Ruhm ertönt aus Millionen Kehlen, da dürfen wir uns wohl freuen, daß der Name des Schiffes, welches jene erste Schaar herübertrug an diese Gestade, gleichsam einen prophetischen Klang hat: "Concord", — Eintracht!—

"Concordia parvæ res crescunt."

Durch Eintracht wuchs das Kleine und sein Gedeihen ist Allen sichtbar. — Ja, „Richte dich auf, Germania!" und vernimm den Jubel deiner Kinder, die dir ein neues Heim begründeten an diesen amerikanischen Gestaden!

Wir jubeln aber nicht bloß als Deutsche, sondern wir jubeln vor allem als Amerikaner. Amerikaner sind wir geworden, freie Bürger dieser großen Republik, und so gute und opferfreudige Bürger, wie nur irgend Einem

Heinrich A. Rattermann delivered the main address during Cincinnati's celebration of the German American bicentennial in 1883. His speech can be found in his collected works, *Gesammelte ausgewählte Werke*, Vol. 16 (1912).

Pictured is a postcard issued for the 225th anniversary of the founding of Germantown, Pennsylvania, the first permanent all-German settlement in America.

In 1983, Gov. Richard F. Celeste appointed the Ohio German American Tricentennial Commission to plan and coordinate the celebration in Ohio, which has a population that is approximately 40 percent of German ancestry, making it the largest ethnic element in the state.

Governor Celeste appointed Jack Wiewel, president of the Federation of German American Societies of Greater Cleveland, as chairman of the Ohio German American Tricentennial Commission.

In commemoration of the tricentennial, the Cincinnati Historical Society published a volume, *Festschrift for the German American Tricentennial Jubilee* (1983), edited by the author of this work.

In commemoration of the tricentennial, the GACL dedicated a plaque in Memorial Hall in Over-the-Rhine to honor Maj. David Ziegler (1748–1811) for his service in the American Revolution and as the first mayor of Cincinnati (1802).

The US Postal Service issued this stamp to commemorate the celebration of the German American tricentennial in 1983; a similar stamp was issued in Germany.

In 1985, the German American Tricentennial Commission issued its final report on the yearlong celebration of the tricentennial in 1983. Numerous events, programs, and celebrations had taken place across the country, engendering a great resurgence of interest as well as pride in the German American heritage.

GERMAN-AMERICAN TRICENTENNIAL
THREE HUNDRED YEARS OF GERMAN IMMIGRATION TO AMERICA
1683 - 1983

FINAL REPORT OF THE PRESIDENTIAL COMMISSION
FOR THE GERMAN-AMERICAN TRICENTENNIAL
TO THE PRESIDENT AND THE CONGRESS OF THE UNITED STATES

1985

During a Rose Garden ceremony at the White House, President Reagan signed the proclamation declaring the sixth of October as German American Day. The author expressed gratitude for his support of the proclamation and also presented him with a copy of one of his books.

THE WHITE HOUSE

WASHINGTON

November 16, 1987

Dear Dr. Tolzman:

It was a pleasure to welcome you, your fellow representatives of major German-American organizations, and members of the government of the Federal Republic of Germany to the White House last month. I was honored to sign the Proclamation declaring October 6 as German-American Day 1987.

For more than three centuries, German-Americans have helped to create the ideas and physical essence of our nation. Today, we continue the historic alliance which we share with the Federal Republic of Germany and are proud of the vast contributions which Americans of German ancestry have made to our society.

I want to thank you for the copy of The Cincinnati Germans After The Great War which you presented to me. I'm pleased to have this volume for my library, and your kind gesture is indeed appreciated.

Nancy joins me in sending you and your membership our best wishes for the future.

Sincerely,

Ronald Reagan

Dr. Don Heinrich Tolzman
President
Society for German-American Studies
University of Cincinnati
Cincinnati, Ohio 45221

President Reagan sent this letter thanking the author for a copy of the book, which is now in the Reagan Presidential Library in California.

In Cincinnati, the declaration of the sixth of October as German American Day was honored with a special celebration on Fountain Square, sponsored by the GACL of Greater Cincinnati.

In October 1989, the first annual German-American Heritage Month in the United States was sponsored by the GACL and organized by the author, who recommended that similar celebrations be held elsewhere. Since that time, the celebration of German-American Heritage Month has spread across the country.

CINCINNATI BOARD OF EDUCATION

OCTOBER GERMAN-AMERICAN HERITAGE MONTH

October has been designated German-American Heritage Month by the Cincinnati Public School Board. Last year at a meeting of the German-American Heritage Committee of the German-American Citizens League it was decided to try to have October set aside to honor German-American Heritage and to provide information so that the youth of our city would come to appreciate and esteem the contributions of our ancestors the early and later immigrants from Germany.

In August 1989 representatives of all the German-American societies and representatives of the German-American Community made a presentation to the Board. Presentations were made by Auguste G. Kent principal of the Tri-State German-American School, David Bitter president of the German-American Citizens League and Don Heinrich Tolzmann president of the German-American Studies Program a the University of Cincinnati.

Notification of the presentation was made in September

A Sourcebook has been prepared and was printed by The Cincinnati Public Schools and made available to each teacher. Additionally the German-American Citizens League printed and distributed the 35 page book to additional area, private grade and high schools.

David Bitter, president of the GACL, went before the Cincinnati Board of Education, successfully requesting that the annual celebration of German-American Heritage Month be included in the public schools of Cincinnati.

German American Heritage Exhibit

a Cincinnati Bicentennial project:
Funded & supported by:

GERMAN-AMERICAN CITIZENS' LEAGUE
DOWNTOWN COUNCIL
FREDERICK HAUCK
FEDERAL REPUBLIC OF GERMANY
FORMICA CORPORATION
PARKWAY PRODUCTS
HARLAN TYPESETTING

research - Don Heinrich Tolzmann
display concept - Nancy Bitter · Charlie Schaupp
display adaptation engineering - Peter Rausch, Frank Kalaney
archival materials and permission to copy-
  University of Cincinnati: Blegen Library, German-Americana Collection
  Atheneum - Archives Archdiocese of Cincinnati
  History of the Archdiocese of Cincinnati 1821-1921
    publisher Fr. Pustet · Rev. John H. Lamott
  Souvenir Album Catholic Churches of Cincinnati and Hamilton County
    Ohio - United States Church Album Publishing Co. 1896
  College of Mount St. Joseph
  Kent State University Press

The celebration of German-American Heritage Month was actively promoted by means of the cultural information booth of the GACL, which was set up at the various festivals in the area throughout the year.

An exhibit prepared for the celebration of Cincinnati's bicentennial in 1988 was widely displayed in the following years during the celebration of German-American Heritage Month and is now on display at the German Heritage Museum.

Since its inception, the governor of Ohio has issued proclamations for the statewide celebration of German-American Heritage Month.

STATE OF OHIO

Executive Department

OFFICE OF THE GOVERNOR

Columbus

RESOLUTION

WHEREAS, the President, Senate and House of Representatives of the United States of America in Proclamation and in an act of Congress officially recognize October 6 as National German American Heritage Day; and

WHEREAS, Ohio is proud to be called home to over 3 million people of Germanic ancestry. From the early days of Ohio's history through this very day in every corner of the State, the Germans who settled in Ohio and their descendants have contributed greatly to the diversity and quality of life through dedication to the values of family, hard work, faith and a solid education, among others; and

WHEREAS, Germans who settled in Ohio and their descendants have contributed greatly to the enrichment of all aspects of life in the State of Ohio and the United States of America, through military and governmental service, medicine, science, education, art, agriculture, business and industry; and

WHEREAS, the State of Ohio recognizes the rich cultural heritage passed along to future generations as they sponsor special events and programs of public education about the language, ethnic heritage and achievements of German citizens.

NOW, THEREFORE, I, BOB TAFT, Governor of the State of Ohio, do hereby designate

October 2003

as

GERMAN AMERICAN HERITAGE MONTH

throughout the State of Ohio and invite all multicultural communities, especially the German American community, to join in appropriate observances and activities throughout this month of celebration and recognition of German culture, music, food and family traditions.

On this 1st day of October, 2003;

Bob Taft

Bob Taft
Governor

German Heritage Month
October 2003

Using Church Records to Uncover Your German Roots

Kenton County Public Library
502 Scott Street
Covington, KY 41011
(859) 962-4060

The public library systems on both sides of the Ohio River participate in the annual celebration of German-American Heritage Month, offering a series of programs, exhibits, and lectures.

Fairview
German-Language
School

Deutsch-amerikanischer Tag
(German-American Day)

Direktorin/Principal: Frau Karen Mulligan
Chor/Choir: Frau Katie Hofmann
Streicher/Orchestra: Frau Melanie Markowich

am 3ten. Oktober 2003

um

9.20 Uhr

und

10.30 Uhr

The Fairview German Language School in Clifton sponsors a German American Day program every year that involves several hundred children from the school.

On October 6, 2008, the 325th anniversary of the founding of Germantown took place in Philadelphia and was coordinated by Marlene Stocks, who chaired the German American Day Committee. The author was invited to present the main address in Philadelphia's Vernon Park, where the Pastorious Monument is located.

Seven

DAUGHTER SETTLEMENTS

In the course of the 19th century, Cincinnati developed not only into "the Queen of the West" but also as a major gateway to the West. It became a destination point for German immigrants and a distribution center for settlement throughout the Ohio Valley, as well as the Midwest in general. This was due to its geographical location as the major city on the Ohio River, where it was conveniently located at the point where rivers converged, which also led to it becoming a center of trade and commerce. German immigrants often came through the Greater Cincinnati area on their way westward by means of the Ohio River.

A number of German American settlement societies were established in Cincinnati that aimed to create German settlements elsewhere. Cincinnati functioned as a point from which migration to other areas took place. The settlements they established might best be referred to as daughter settlements. Many have maintained ongoing connections and relations to the Greater Cincinnati area, existing to this day.

Located about two hours north of Cincinnati and west of I-75 is the town of Minster, which was settled in 1832 by a group of German immigrants under the leadership of Franz Joseph Stallo. Originally known as Stallostown, the village was incorporated in 1839 as Minster. Like many other towns in the region, the immigration was from northwestern Germany.

West of Cincinnati and a bit to the north of I-75 is the town of Oldenburg, which, as its name reflects, was settled in 1837 by German immigrants from northwestern Germany, where Oldenburg is located. Upon entering the town, one notices that the streets all have signs with German names.

New Ulm, Minnesota, has strong ties with Cincinnati. Founded in 1854 by Germans from Chicago, the settlement was then acquired by members of the Cincinnati Turnverein. It came to be known as a Turnerstadt, or a Turner Town.

All three of these towns provide examples of settlements founded by Germans from Cincinnati and may justifiably be viewed as daughter settlements.

Minster, Ohio, was originally named for Franz Joseph Stallo (1792–1833), who arrived in Cincinnati in 1831 from Damme in northwestern Germany. He wrote letters attracting German immigrants from the Osnabrück area, which resulted in the formation of a settlement society, led by Stallo, in Cincinnati.

This is a centennial history, published in 1932, that provides a pictorial and documentary history of the first century of Minster, Ohio, including genealogical information on the Stallo family.

After the death of Stallo, the town was renamed Minster (1836). In the meantime, the construction of the Miami-Erie Canal was underway, connecting Lake Erie to the north with the Ohio River to the south, and in 1843, the first canal boat reached the town.

Construction of the St. Augustine Church in Minster began in 1848 and was completed in 1850. Buildings were added for the convent and school, as well.

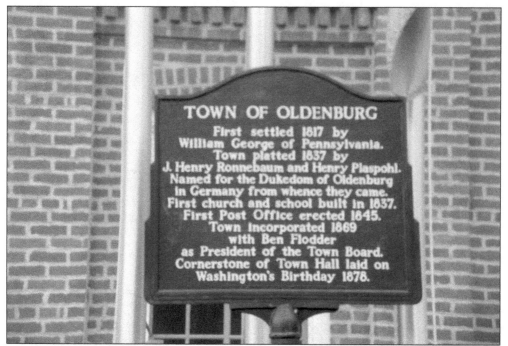

A historical marker in Oldenburg, Indiana, provides information about the two German immigrants who laid out the plat plan for the town, naming it after the province they came from, the Dukedom of Oldenburg.

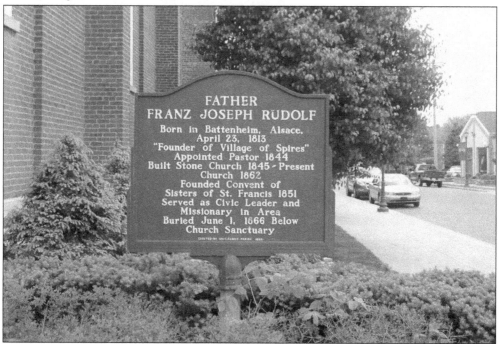

Fr. Franz Joseph Rudolf (1813–1866) is considered the "Father of the Village of Spires," as Oldenburg is known. In addition to the Holy Family Church, the Franciscan Monastery and the Immaculate Conception Convent and Academy were also constructed there.

Hochw. Franziskus Joseph Rudolf.

Fr. Franz Joseph Rudolf was appointed pastor of Oldenburg in 1844, becoming the spiritual leader, as well as the community leader.

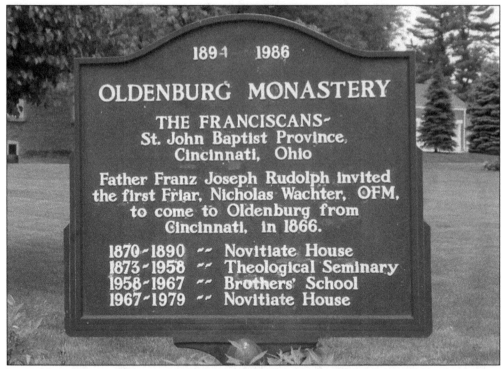

189? 1986

OLDENBURG MONASTERY

THE FRANCISCANS-
St. John Baptist Province,
Cincinnati, Ohio

Father Franz Joseph Rudolph invited
the first Friar, Nicholas Wachter, OFM,
to come to Oldenburg from
Cincinnati, in 1866.

1870-1890 ~~ Novitiate House
1873-1958 ~~ Theological Seminary
1958-1967 ~~ Brothers' School
1967-1979 ~~ Novitiate House

In 1866, Father Rudolf invited the first of the Franciscans to come to Oldenburg from nearby Cincinnati.

The Holy Name Church towers over the town of Oldenburg. The church was built in the Gothic style in 1862. In 1919, stained glass windows from Germany were installed. The church contains a crypt where Father Rudolf is buried.

The Johanniter-Halle originally served as headquarters for the Knights of St. John in Oldenburg. Buildings with German signs can be found throughout the town of Oldenburg and highlight the German heritage of the area.

German street signs are found on every corner in Oldenburg, paying tribute to the town's German heritage. Many other towns and cities in the country lost their German street names during World War I as a result of the anti-German hysteria of the time. Towns and cities like Cincinnati and Oldenburg have set a good example by returning German street signs to the landscape.

Pictured is the sign for a popular pub in Oldenburg.

Many stone houses and buildings can be found in Oldenburg.

New Ulm was first settled in 1854 by a group of Germans from Chicago who were led by Ferdinand Beinhorn. By the time this postcard appeared (around 1910), the settlement had developed into a thriving community.

Col. Wilhelm Pfaender, president of the Turner Settlement Society of Cincinnati, visited New Ulm in 1856, resulting in the sale of the townsite to the Turners. The first group of Germans from Cincinnati followed in September 1856 with more arriving in the spring of 1857.

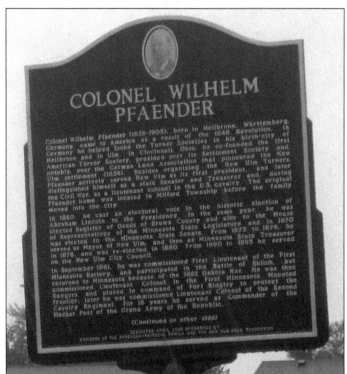

A historical marker in honor of Col. Wilhelm Pfaender was recently dedicated in New Ulm. (Courtesy of Marge and Pete Poole.)

The first Turner Hall in New Ulm (1857) was burnt to the ground during the Sioux Uprising of 1862. In 1873, this building was constructed to take its place. A wide variety of programs and activities are held at Turner Hall, which also includes an excellent restaurant.

Capt. Jacob Nix (1822–1897) came to America after participating in the Revolutions of 1848 in Germany and supported Pfaender's idea of establishing a German settlement on the frontier, settling there with his family in 1858. During the Sioux Uprising of 1862, he served as commandant for the first battle of New Ulm.

The German-Bohemian Heritage Monument pays tribute to the large number of German Bohemian immigrants who settled in New Ulm and surrounding Brown County. (Courtesy of Marge and Pete Poole.)

The Hermann Monument in New Ulm is situated on a hillside overlooking the city. Dedicated in 1897, it was placed in the National Register of Historic Places in 1973, and in 2000, the US Congress designated it as the official symbol for German contributions to America. (Courtesy of Marge and Pete Poole.)

Brick stones and pavers line the walkway leading to the Hermann Monument in New Ulm, several of which were placed by Cincinnatians with New Ulm connections, including the author of this volume. (Courtesy of Marge and Pete Poole.)

IN MEMORY OF
E. H. TOLZMANN
103 YEARS

DR. D.H. TOLZMANN
UND FAMILIE

Turner Hall in New Ulm is the oldest such hall in the country, with the oldest part of the building dating to 1873. It was designed by New Ulm architect Julius Berndt, who is known as the father of the Hermann Monument, as he also designed that.

J.H. Strasser (1855–1914) served as editor and publisher of a German-language newspaper, the *New Ulm Post*, and wrote a valuable history and chronology of the city that is now available in English translation as *New Ulm, Minnesota: J.H. Strasser's History and Chronology*. It was translated and edited by the author of this volume.

Eight

GERMAN HERITAGE
MUSEUM

A welcome addition on the museum landscape in the Greater Cincinnati area is the German Heritage Museum, established by the GACL and opened in September 2000. Due to its location, it focuses on German immigration, settlement, and influences in the Ohio Valley. However, it also takes a national focus with exhibits covering the entire range of German American history, including displays on German Americans in the American Revolution.

The museum came about as a result of the centennial celebration of the GACL in 1995. To mark the event, the museum would be established. Pleasantly located in Green Township's West Fork Park, the German Heritage Museum has become a major attraction in the Greater Cincinnati area. It has playground and picnic facilities and a wooded area with walking trails.

The museum itself consists of a 19th-century log house that belonged to the Feist family for more than 130 years. After the last resident of the log house died, the building was donated to the GACL, which felt that it best represented the typical home of a German pioneer farm family in the area. This was considered important, as the home of a well-to-do person, such as a mansion, would not have represented or related to the common German American experience of the German pioneers who settled the area.

The German Heritage Museum sponsors several events throughout the year, including Maifest, the St. Nikolaus Day celebration, and the German Heritage Museum lecture series. An active educational outreach program brings students from schools, colleges, and universities. Visitors from across the country and from Europe are welcomed throughout the year, including diplomatic representatives, such as the German ambassador.

The German Heritage Museum is housed in a German-style log house that belonged to the Feist family. Included in this image are the following: Philipp Feist (seated in the center) with his wife, Caroline, seven sons, and four daughters. Feist came to America in 1855 from Baden-Baden, and settled in Cincinnati. In 1865, he purchased a farm with the log house in Delhi Township. Later in the 19th century, the house was covered with siding.

Members of the Feist family lived in the log house from 1865 to 1994. After the death of the last member of the family resident on the farm, the building was dismantled, and the log house underneath the siding was discovered. It was donated to the GACL, which reassembled and refurbished the structure to house the German Heritage Museum.

After obtaining the log house, ground-breaking ceremonies were held at West Fork Park in Green Township. Featured here are, from left to right, August Pust, representative of governor George Voinovich of Ohio; Dr. Don Heinrich Tolzmann, GACL president; Elmer Grossheim, GACL Museum Building Committee chairman; Tony Upton, Green Township trustee; and Congressman Steve Chabot.

After the construction work was completed, the German Heritage Museum was dedicated on September 23, 2000, and has attracted an ever-growing number of visitors from the region, the United States, and the German-speaking countries of Europe. Special guests have included Wolfgang Ischinger, German ambassador to the United States, and Col. Gail Halvorsen, well known as the "Candy Bomber" during the Berlin airlift.

The German Heritage Museum is in West Fork Park in Green Township, on the west side of Cincinnati near I-74. (Courtesy of Dykstra Photography.)

The German Heritage Brick Walk contains bricks with the names of the societies and individuals who donated funds for the construction of the museum. (Courtesy of Dykstra Photography.)

This pedestal, once on Fountain Square, was moved to the German Heritage Museum in 2005 as the inscription became dated after the renovation of the fountain in 2000. Nevertheless, it contains information on the past history of the fountain, indicating that it was cast by the Royal Bronze Foundry in Munich.

A defining feature of a German-style log house is the central chimney; log cabins built by non-Germans usually had the chimney at either end of the building. The advantage of a central chimney is that it can heat the entire building, while a fireplace at the end of the building would only heat that area of the building. (Courtesy of Dykstra Photography.)

This exhibit case displays some of the rare German-language books at the museum and a picture of Heinrich A. Rattermann, who organized the first German Day in 1895 and is considered the founding father of the organization that sponsors the museum, the GACL. (Courtesy of Dykstra Photography.)

This room displays a cross from the Third German Protestant Memorial Church, a table from the German Baptist Church, and a collection of German and German American books that belonged to members of the German American community of the area. (Courtesy of Dykstra Photography.)

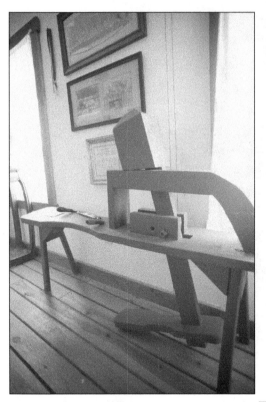

This Schnitzelbank, or woodcarving bench, was built by John Klein, a well-known German American woodcarver in Cincinnati. His carving of the *Guardian Angel* is also on display at the museum. (Courtesy of Dykstra Photography.)

This spinning wheel from Löningen, Germany, was brought to Cincinnati by the Schwegmann family and was donated to the museum by Margaret Froehlich. (Courtesy of Dykstra Photography.)

This immigrant trunk belonged to Gottlieb Bauer (1844–1909), who brought it with him from a small village near Stuttgart when he came to America. It was donated to the museum by the Kentuckiana German Heritage Society. (Courtesy of Dykstra Photography.)

Wooden shoes were brought to Cincinnati by German immigrants from northwestern Germany. Since many German gardeners were employed at Spring Grove Cemetery, a neighborhood arose alongside it known as Wooden Shoe Hollow. (Courtesy of Dykstra Photography.)

The original flag of the GACL is on display at the German Heritage Museum and was preserved and framed as a donation from Gottfried and Josephine Schlembach. (Courtesy of Dykstra Photography.)

The crest of the German Heritage Museum includes the American and German eagles as symbols of German American heritage.

FOR FURTHER READING

German Cincinnati Revisited is a follow-up to the author's earlier volume, *German Cincinnati* (Charleston, S.C.: Arcadia Publishing, 2005). For further information on the region, see also the author's *German Heritage Guide to the Greater Cincinnati Area.* 2nd ed. (Milford, Ohio: Little Miami Publishing Co., 2003), and Gustav Koerner's *The German Element in the Ohio Valley: Ohio, Kentucky, and Indiana,* translated and edited by Don Heinrich Tolzmann (Baltimore, Maryland: Genealogical Publishing Co., 2011).

Also, see the author's *German Americana: Selected Essays* (Milford, Ohio: Little Miami Publishing Co., 2009), and the website, www.donheinrichtolzmann.net for references to other works dealing with German American history and culture.

www.arcadiapublishing.com

Discover books about the town where you grew up, the cities where your friends and families live, the town where your parents met, or even that retirement spot you've been dreaming about. Our Web site provides history lovers with exclusive deals, advanced notification about new titles, e-mail alerts of author events, and much more.

MADE IN THE

Arcadia Publishing, the leading local history publisher in the United States, is committed to making history accessible and meaningful through publishing books that celebrate and preserve the heritage of America's people and places. Consistent with our mission to preserve history on a local level, this book was printed in South Carolina on American-made paper and manufactured entirely in the United States.

This book carries the accredited Forest Stewardship Council (FSC) label and is printed on 100 percent FSC-certified paper. Products carrying the FSC label are independently certified to assure consumers that they come from forests that are managed to meet the social, economic, and ecological needs of present and future generations.

FSC
Mixed Sources
Product group from well-managed forests and other controlled sources

Cert no. SW-COC-001530
www.fsc.org
© 1996 Forest Stewardship Council

Find Your Place in History.

9 781531 655167